AF430272

TITLE PAGE

Real Estate

Real Estate Investing

Ebuka Ugboma

COPYRIGHT

DISCLAIMER

This material is not meant to serve as a substitute for professional financial or legal counsel. No changes to a financial plan or strategy should be made without first discussing the matter with an expert. Neither the publisher nor the Author makes any promises about the amount of money you will make using this method.

TABLE OF CONTENT

DEDICATION

This work is dedicated to my wonderful children; chioma and chimemelie

ACKNOWLEDGEMENT

I hereby acknowledge the contributions of my past University Lecturers on Real Estates Law, Property Law, Land Law, Property Law and Practice. You are the greatest minds on Real Estate.

ABOUT THE AUTHOR

Gary Austine Ebuka Ugboma Esq FICMC, ACIArb UK, FMA, AGIS, PMP

LLB Hons, BA Hons, Dip Mus Ed, Pdip Bus Admin, PDip Estate Mgt, MBA, MSC Peace and conflict resolution.

Ebuka Ugboma has multiple degrees from different Universities across different fields; Arts, Law, Social Sciences and Humanities generally. He is a Chartered Arbitrator and Mediator, trained in the style and pattern of Chartered Institute Of Arbitrators UK.

Ebuka Ugboma has successfully published many books including Propensities And Habits For Success

Check out and buy his books on Amazon:

https://www.amazon.com/Ebuka-Ugboma/e/B0B6HHVVW6

Email: garyugboma@gmail.com Phone: 2348033924157

Chapter One

Introduction

Real estate can be a very lucrative market, and investors can make a lot of money in the process. Investing in real estate also benefits local communities as long as there is an industry of skilled workers available to buy or sell property. Not only does this benefit the economy, but it also brings some much-needed modernization to areas that are otherwise limited by time and space.

Because there are so many real estate companies out there, finding the right company for you can be confusing and overwhelming! That's why we've put together this post all about how to succeed in "real estate" (a more general term) no matter where you live.

Who is this guide for?

This guide is for anyone looking to invest in real estate. First and foremost, it's for people who want to invest in "commercial properties", meaning properties that are meant for businesses or companies. Real estate companies have used terminology such as "Retail Foreclosures" to describe properties that are fit only for retail stores, and "Residential Properties" to describe homes. We'll go into more detail below, but when you're looking at investing in any kind of property, always look out for these terms on the site; that way you can buy with confidence knowing exactly what kind of property you're buying.

Chapter Two

What Is Meant By A Real Estate?

A "real estate" is any kind of property that can be bought and sold for investment or personal gain. Examples include houses, land, commercial spaces and more. The term primarily refers to the investing market in general. It's less common to hear people referring to "the real estate" when they mean the industry as a whole, like how we might talk about the movie industry as "the film business". We'll look at the four main kinds of real estate in this article; commercial properties, residential properties, retail foreclosures and lease-to-own contracts.

What Is The Main Concept Of Real Estate?

Real estate is a tough market to invest in because there are a lot of different ways to approach it. One could invest in property as an investor, where you simply buy and sell the same property multiple times. This involves using your capital (invested money) as soon as you're able to make another purchase, hoping that at some point in the future, you'll end up making a profit on that investment. Typically speaking, investors buy low and sell high; they purchase high value properties and then rent them out while they wait for the market to bounce back even higher.

Another way to invest in real estate is through a "developer" or "contractor". This is where you either build a property from scratch or buy one that's already built by someone else. When you buy a lot, you're buying an empty plot of land and then building your own house on it. When you buy an existing property, it could be an apartment, townhouse or other kind of dwelling unit.

In both of these cases, you're buying a lot of value in the form of potential with very little risk involved. The price you pay for a lot or apartment could increase over time and/or you can use it to build value in other areas of your life, so long as you continue to rent it out. However, even if the properties don't increase in value or if you choose to sell them, they'll still be creating income for years to come by renting them out.

You could also invest in real estate property by "leasing" the property that's already yours. In this case, you wouldn't buy the property yourself but would instead rent it out to another individual, who would then manage and upkeep the property while they continue paying their rent each month. You'd then receive a portion of the money from each rental payment as profit.

It's important to note that when you're buying properties, whether it be a lot or an apartment, "assignments" often come with the property. This means that even if you sell it later, someone else will still be living there. That said, owning property will give you an asset that can grow in value over time.

Why Has Every Market Crashed?

This is actually a very good question! With the global housing market exploding at a rate never seen before, it's no surprise that prices have skyrocketed and that crash has caused people to lose faith in real estate altogether. There are many potential reasons why this could happen; one of the main ones is legislation and regulation.

When you invest in a lot, an apartment or any other kind of property, you're not just buying the building itself. You're also buying land. This is why we often hear people say that the value of property is much, much higher than the cost of the actual building. This means that if you buy a $100 000 Apartment but then discover that the land it was built on was worth three times more than that, you'll be missing out on a lot of money!

One example of this happening would be to look at government regulation on private land ownerships. For example, many countries like the US or UK have strict laws surrounding what kind of use can be made of a piece of land. Any use that isn't allowed by the government may negatively affect you in some way and could result in "civil" actions; for example, if you rent out your property to someone and they decide to build a large house on the land, yet only your building was allowed by the government. In this case, they would probably build a slightly smaller house on the same piece of land and then sue you for not getting any part of that property.

These kinds of laws commonly affect a lot of people in all areas of the world, but are especially prevalent in the developing countries. We can't, for example, go around building massive houses on land and then selling them to Chinese investors or Russian investors who don't know how to deal with the stringent laws in their own country. Unless you live in those countries yourself, you won't be able to participate in this type of activity.

Another way that legislation and regulations can negatively impact your property is through zoning requirements . This is where local governments put restrictions on what kind of use you're allowed to make for a specific property. In some cases, this could mean that you can't build a large house specifically for the purpose of renting it out or selling it. If you're renting it from someone, often the government will force you to live in the house and then only allow for a certain number of guests to be allowed in the property. This is different than if you owned your own place and had to rent it out because there's no way you can fit everyone in your living quarters.

As an investor, one way that this can negatively affect you is if you're planning on selling your property soon but are worried about being forced out by a government official who claims that they think that building a larger home "will cause harm" to the neighborhood. This is why it's a good idea to know what kind of policies the government has in place when you're trying to get involved in real estate.

Chapter Three

Where To Get Started

The best way to get started with this is by looking online. Google "property for sale" and see what kind of results you can find. If you'd like, for safety purposes, this can also be done offline at your local property market. It might be a good idea, however, if you're looking for specific properties to contact an agent and get a quote before making any commitments because sometimes sites like Google or Zillow won't include all the properties on offer.

There are also seminars, like Zillow Seminars and other real estate investment seminars that can be found all around the world. If you're interested in participating in any of these, please use caution. You should always read up on the company before you buy into anything and make sure to ask questions . You can also find a lot of information by contacting your local realtors who can work with you on finding the best properties and keeping you updated on any new properties that come up for sale in the area.

This is probably one of the best methods that anyone can use to try and start investing in real estate, although it's not often as profitable as buying a single property outright.

If you're looking for information about certain properties, it's always better to ask (in person) about a place you're interested in rather than doing background research online. If possible, have a conversation with someone who owns something similar to the property you're looking for and ask them about their experience with it; whether it was positive or negative. If the person was able to make money off of the property, ask them about how long it took them to do so. This will give you a good idea of how well they understand the investment. From there, if you feel comfortable investing in them, you can ask for more information about the property and what they did to make it turn out so well.

Real Estate Investing as a Hobby

The first thing that everyone has to remember while they are trying to get into investing in real estate is that it is NOT a good idea to do this as a hobby. One of the main reasons why is because eventually, you'll start putting some money into buying properties and managing your portfolio, which could slow down your income stream significantly.

What can you do instead?

If you do want to try this, I suggest looking at it as a hobby. Sure, you'll probably lose money for quite some time before any real cash starts rolling in, but I think it could be a fun thing to do and that the experience of investing in real estate can come in handy many times down the road . Why is this? Well, unfortunately, not everyone who buys a property ends up being able to sell it consistently. Sometimes, for any number of reasons, a deal doesn't go through and the property ends up being left sitting on the market for quite a while. In this case, even if you have enough money to continue buying properties, you might not be able to sell them . This is where it can be nice to have some experience in real estate because you can either use those properties as collateral for more purchases or use the money made from the previous deal to make more deals that you can sell.

If it's just a hobby that you want to be involved with, however, I would recommend looking at buying an apartment building or trying out some other small-scale venture like selling T-shirts online.

Real Estate Investing as a Business

If it's not just a hobby that you want to get into, I think it can be very interesting to try and start investing in real estate as a business . Why is this? Well, if you wanted to make most of your money off of investing real estate, the first thing that would come to your mind would probably be buying single-family homes. However, the problem with this is that the rules on sale are different when you're dealing with individual properties (as opposed to apartment buildings or retail spaces). This can make it difficult if not impossible at times because you could end up finding yourself unable to make much money off of these properties.

Another reason why it might be a good idea to try and do this as a business is because if you're looking to fund your retirement, it can be much easier to make long-term goals with a business than it could be with something that's considered a hobby. How is this? Well, let's say that you wanted $1 million dollars for the property. If you go about this as a hobby, that would mean that you would have to invest $1 million just to get started. However, if you're doing this as a business, in order for your business to break even, all you would have to do is find $500,000 worth of properties that you can invest in and sell for at least the same amount.

How to get started

First things first, you have to decide whether or not you want to do this as a business or just as a hobby. If it's just a hobby, you'll have more time for other important things like learning real estate investing strategies and investing in new properties. If it's going to be a business, however (and this is where most people start), you'll want to get your business up and running so that it can actually break even; meaning that all of the expenses will be covered by the profits.

Setting up your own company can be done online and will allow you to do many of the things that companies normally do such as manage finances online and take payments online. If you're planning on doing this as a business, here are some of the things that you'll want to do first:

1. Register your company.

2. Get a legal business name. You can do this by searching online or perhaps looking in the white pages (for the United States).

3. Find an accountant that offers real estate investing at a reasonable rate to help with everything from taxes to bookkeeping and auditing.

4. Start looking for properties. This is probably the most important thing that you'll have to do. Make sure that you're doing your due diligence on the properties and that you're buying something that's not only structurally sound but also something where the price is right.

5. It's a good idea to have a lawyer in your corner who understands real estate investing as well because it could save you trouble later on down the road. This is especially important when it comes to setting up LLCs and other business organization types as well as handling contracts and paperwork .

6. Don't forget to advertise your property and make sure that you have money in your escrow account so that you can start taking payments right away.

7. Most importantly, be sure to not only get as much work done on the property as possible before it even goes on the market, but also continue working on it after it's up for sale.

Chapter Four

CONCLUSION

The more people who are successful at it -- financially and otherwise -- the more people will be willing to invest in properties.... which will lead to more properties being sold.... which will lead to more people getting into real estate investing.... and so on and so forth. The most important thing to keep in mind is that it's not easy by any means and that it requires a lot of work up front. However, you have to ask yourself if it's worth it if you could end up taking advantage of the 3% rule or even build yourself a nice little portfolio of 5-10 properties.

It might not be an immediate source of funding, but it can end up being a great way to start building a new stream of income as well as supplement your bank account and retirement account. Most importantly, it might just turn out to be the best real estate investment that you've ever made.

Real Estate Investing For Beginners - What You Need To Get
Started!

In this book, we've talked about the different types of properties
that you can invest in, explained the advantages and disadvantages
to each one, and then gave you specific tactics to use in order to
find opportunities that will make the most sense for you. It's
important to remember that real estate investing isn't for everyone,
and it definitely takes a little bit of money as well as a strong
stomach for risk. However, if you're looking for a new way to
create your own passive income stream then this might just be
what you've been searching for.

In this book, I've also covered some of the basics of how you get
started with real estate investing. There are many different ways to
go about it and your options are going to be limited based on the

type of property that you want to invest in and your personal situation. But whether you want to flip homes, invest in apartments, or even get into some commercial properties, the information that you've received in this book should help make things much clearer for you.

It's a lot of hard work but if you're willing to put in the time and effort then there is a lot to gain from taking advantage of these smart tactics when it comes time for you to make an investment in real estate.

I hope that this book has helped you to gain a better understanding of how the real estate market actually functions and I'm looking forward to hearing your feedback.

...